DK WORKBOOKS

K Math

Author Linda Ruggieri
Educational Consultant Alison Tribley

DK | Penguin Random House

US Editor Allison Singer
US Educational Consultant Alison Tribley
Senior Editors Fran Baines, Cécile Landau
Managing Art Editor Richard Czapnik
Senior Designer Marisa Renzullo
Art Director Martin Wilson
Pre-production Editor Francesca Wardell

DK Delhi
Editor Nandini Gupta
Art Editors Dheeraj Arora, Rashika Kachroo
DTP Designer Anita Yadav
Dy. Managing Editor Soma B. Chowdhury

First American Edition, 2014
Published in the United States by DK Publishing
1450 Broadway, Suite 801, New York, NY 10018

Copyright © 2014 Dorling Kindersley Limited
DK, a Division of Penguin Random House LLC
23 22 21 20 10 9 8 7 6 5
005–197335–02/2014

A catalog record for this book
is available from the Library of Congress.
ISBN: 978-1-4654-1732-9

DK books are available at special discounts
when purchased in bulk for sales promotions,
premiums, fund-raising, or educational use.
For details, contact:
DK Publishing Special Markets
1450 Broadway, Suite 801, New York, NY 10018
or SpecialSales@dk.com

Printed and bound in Canada.

All images © Dorling Kindersley Limited
For further information see: www.dkimages.com

A WORLD OF IDEAS:
SEE ALL THERE IS TO KNOW
www.dk.com

Contents

This chart lists all the topics
in the *book*.

GOAL

Practice counting from 1 to 5.

1 2 3 4 5

How many stars are there in each row?
Circle the correct number.

 ★ ★   2 3 4

★ ★ ★ ★   2 3 4

★ ★ ★   1 2 3

★ ★ ★ ★ ★   3 4 5

Write the two missing numbers on each line.

1   2   [ ]   4   [ ]

[ ]   2   3   [ ]   5

1   [ ]   3   4   [ ]

Practice counting from 6 to 10.

6 7 8 9 10

How many apples are there in each row?
Circle the correct number.

  5 6 7

5 6 7

6 7 8

  5 8 9

6 8 10

Circle any ten flowers below.

GOAL

Practice counting from 10 to 15.

10 11 12 13 14 15

How many objects are there in each box?
Write the correct number.

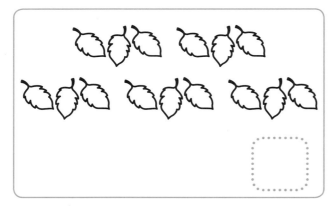

Write the missing numbers in the boxes.

1 ⬚ 3   4 ⬚ 6

7 ⬚ 9   10 ⬚ 12

13 ⬚ 15

1234567891234567891

Practice counting up to 20.

15 16 17 18 19 20

GOAL

Look at the twenty houses along the trail. Write the numbers that are missing in the circle next to each house.

Count twenty doors. Cross out extra doors.
Then write the number 20 in the box.

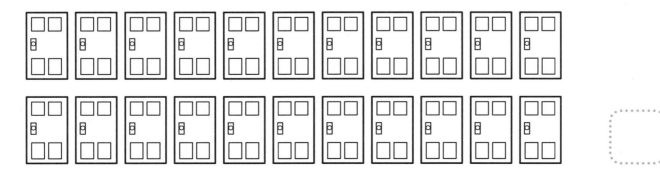

GOAL

Add different numbers from 1 to 9 to make 10.

Count each group of toys. Write the correct number of toys in the box.

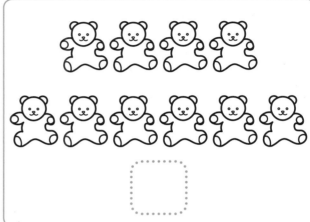

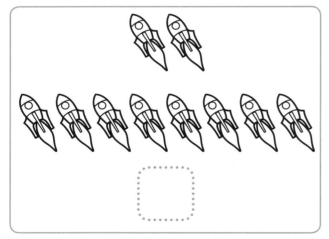

Copy the pattern of dots on the other side of the domino.

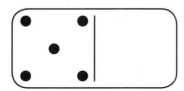

Now count all the dots on the domino, and write the correct number.

  1 2 3 4 5 6 7 8 9 1 2 3 4 5 6 7 8 9 1 2

Review how to make 10.

Write the numbers from 1 to 10 in the circles next to each car on the path below.

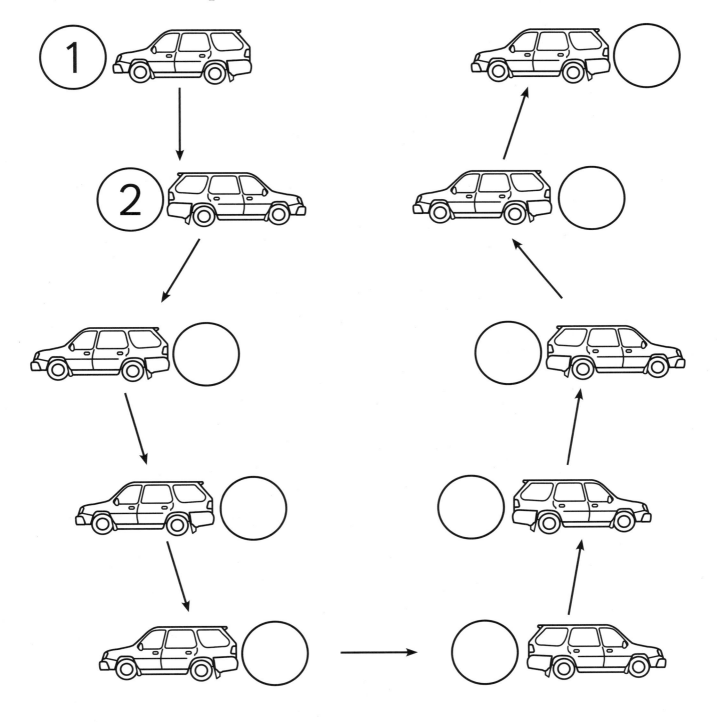

GOAL

Learn about items in groups that make 20.

Count the objects in each box and answer the questions below.

How many boats are there? ⬚

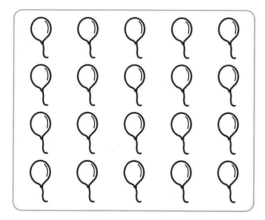

How many balloons are there?

⬚

How many birds are there?

⬚

123456789123456789 12

Review ways to make 20, such as 10 + 10.

Solve these equations.

6 + 14 =	9 + 11 =	8 + 12 =
5 + 15 =	3 + 17 =	16 + 4 =
13 + 7 =	18 + 2 =	19 + 1 =

Circle the equation that adds up to 20.

12 + 4 + 6   5 + 5 + 10   4 + 4 + 9

Follow the path to the castle and write the missing numbers on each stone.

Castle

Learn that objects have shapes, and shapes have names.

Look at the objects. Circle the correct shape of the object in each row.

 The cookie has the shape of a square circle

 The door has the shape of a rectangle triangle

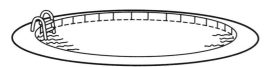 The pool has the shape of an square  oval

 The tree has the shape of a circle triangle

Circle the word to describe the shape of this ball.

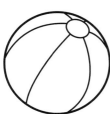   square   circle   triangle

Learn to identify different shapes.

Look at the shapes in each row. Circle the shape that is different.

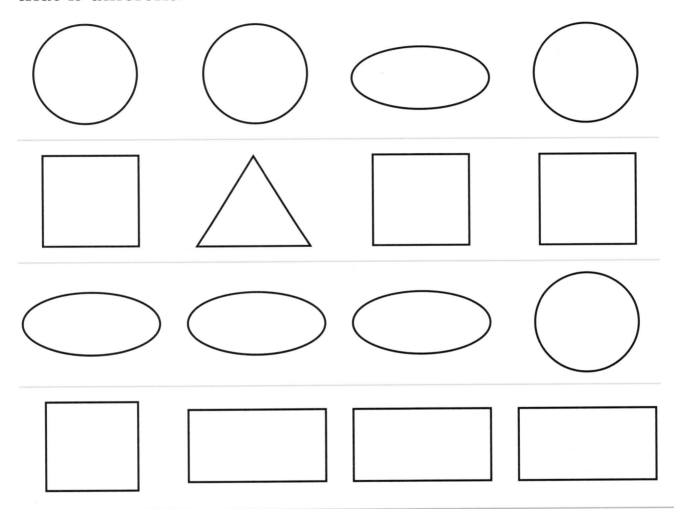

Draw five triangles below. Then draw a silly face on each one.

GOAL Describe shapes by the number of sides and corners.

Circle the word that correctly completes each sentence.

A square has four corners
and .... sides.

three   four

A circle is ....

round   straight

A rectangle has four
corners and is ....

round   long

A triangle has three corners
and .... sides.

two   three

Circle the triangle that is larger than the others.

 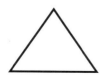 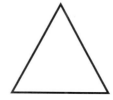 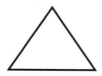

Shapes can vary in size. Learn to find the shapes that are larger.

Look at the shapes in each box. Color in the largest shape.

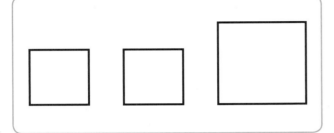

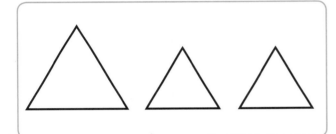
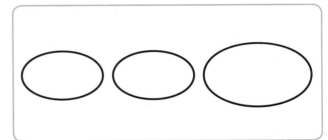

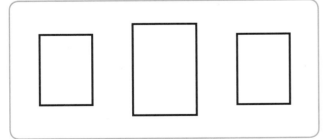
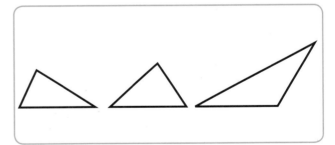

Circle the shape that has four sides.

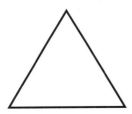
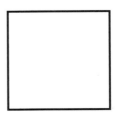

GOAL

Learn to draw shapes.

Look at each shape and make it into an object.

Draw a circle and make it into the sun.

Draw a square and make it into a present.

Draw a triangle and make it into a hat.

Draw an oval and make it into a face.

Practice finding and counting shapes.

Color the circles red. ○   Color the rectangles yellow.

Color the squares blue. ☐   Color the triangles green. △

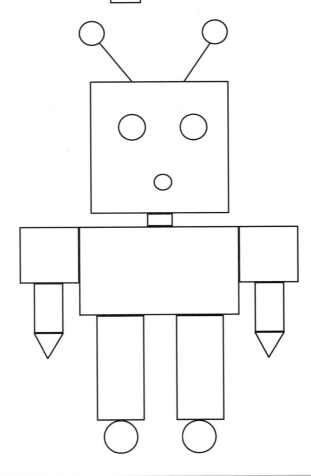

How many of each shape is there in the robot?
Write the correct numbers in the boxes below.

[ ] squares   [ ] circles

[ ] triangles   [ ] rectangles

Learn to draw shapes and continue patterns.
Patterns are repeated sets of objects.

Draw the shape to continue the pattern in each row.

....

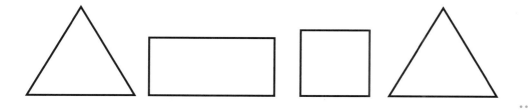

....

....

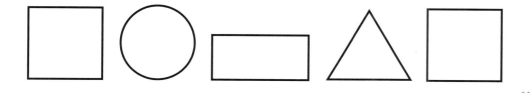

....

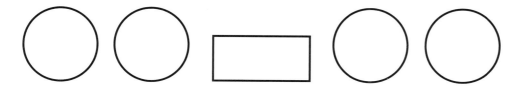

....

GOAL

Practice continuing patterns.

Look at the cupcakes below. In each row, follow the pattern and decorate the tops of the undecorated cupcakes with the correct design.

Look at the pattern of the cookies below. Draw two more cookies to continue the pattern.

Learn to identify objects that are the same.

Look at each row of animals. Circle the two animals that are the same.

Circle the two fish that have the same number on them.

123456789123456789 12

Learn to compare characteristics, such as numbers and letters.

Put the balls into the correct boxes: Draw a line from each ball with a number on it to the number box. Draw a line from each ball with a letter on it to the letter box.

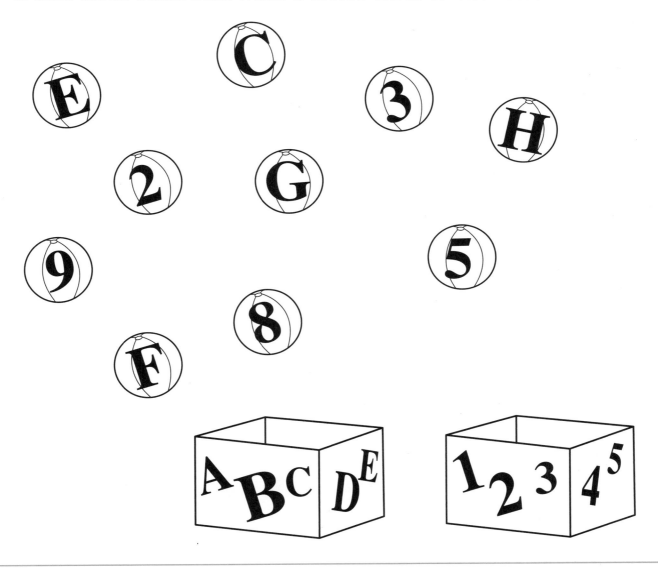

How many balls are there altogether?

GOAL

Learn to find things that are not the same, or different.

Circle the leaf in each row that is different.

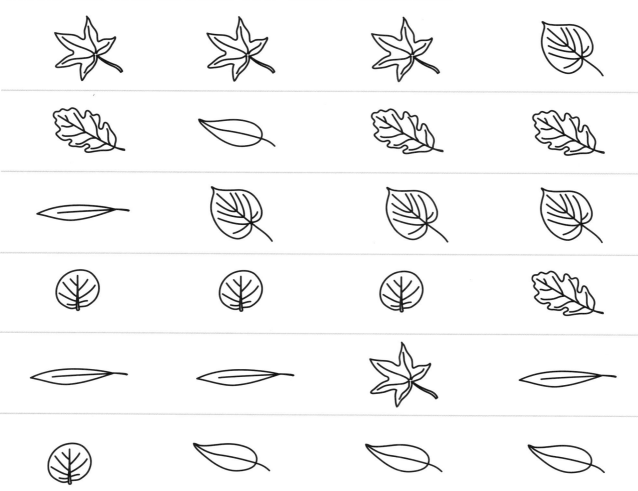

Circle the six flowers that are the same.

Learn to identify (spot) which is different.

Circle the animal in each row that is different.

Add spots to the frog on the right to make the two frogs look the same.

GOAL

Count the objects to find out which set has more.

Write the letter **M** on the line under the box that has more objects.

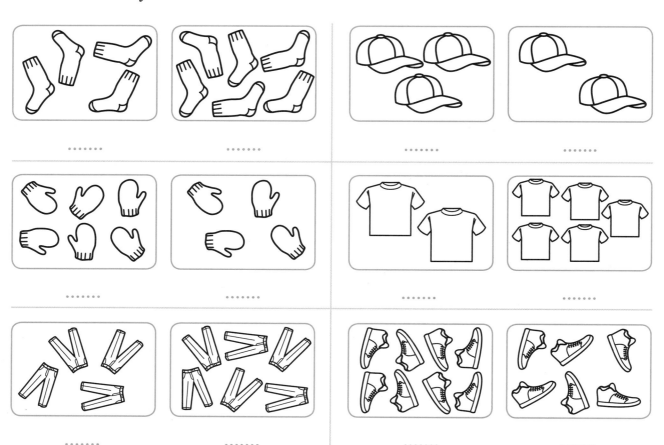

....

....

....

How many sneakers are there below? To find out, count how many are in each pair, then add up the numbers.

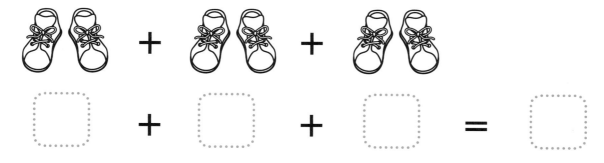

.... + ... + ... = ...

Learn to add one more.

Add one more to each group in the boxes. Then count the total items in the group and write the correct number.

Draw one more balloon, then count the balloons.
How many are there altogether?

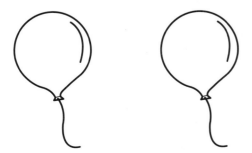

1 2 3 4 5 6 7 8 9 1 2 3 4 5 6 7 8 9 1 2

GOAL

Draw more shapes to add to the group. The + sign means to add.

$\bigcirc + \bigcirc\bigcirc = 3$

Draw two more of the same shape in each box. Then add all the shapes and write the correct number.

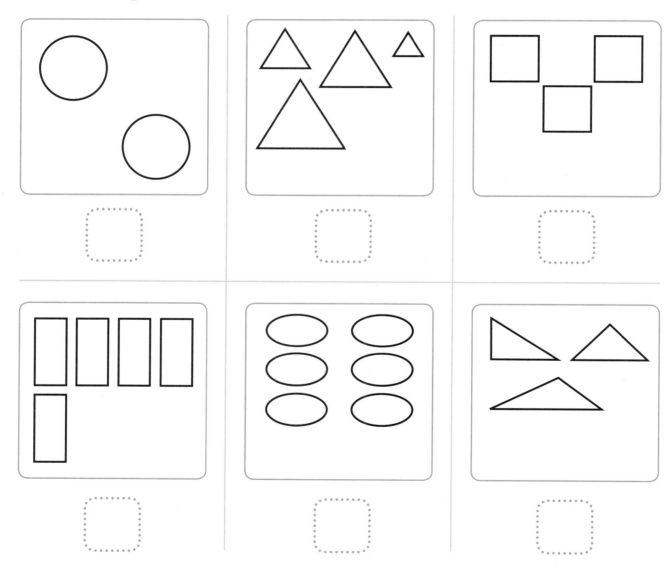

How many triangles are there on this page? Circle the answer.

7   9   11

1234567891234567891 2

Find the total, which is the answer you get when you add things together.  = 6

Draw a + sign between the boxes in each row. Then count all the items in both of the boxes and write the total number.

 =

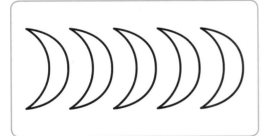 =

 =

In total, how many moons and stars are there on this page? Circle the answer.

12   14   17

Find the group that has fewer objects.

Look at the baked goods below. For each treat, circle the group that has fewer than the other.

cakes

cupcakes

cookies

pies

Count all the cupcakes above. How many are there?

1 2 3 4 5 6 7 8 9 1 2 3 4 5 6 7 8 9 1 2

Take away one object so that a group has one fewer.  2

Look at the pictures in each row. Cross out one of the pictures. Then count the remaining pictures and write the correct number in the box.
Remember: Do not count the picture with the X on it.

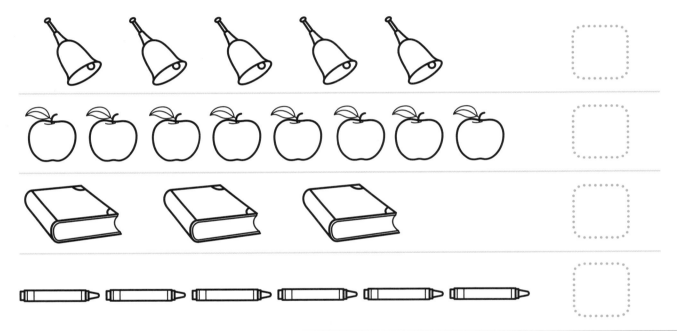

Count the cups below that are not crossed out.
Circle the correct number.

9   15   19

Cross out to show taking away more than one. Count to find how many are left.

Cross out two vegetables in each row. Then count how many are left. Write the correct number in the box.
Remember: Do not count the vegetables you crossed out.

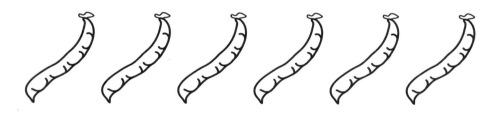

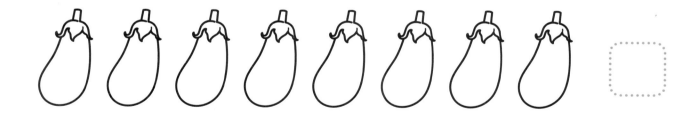

Read the counting poem below. Write the words to complete the poem.

One potato, two potato, ... potato, four!

Five potato, ... potato, seven potato, more!

Cross out three of the animals in each box to

Practice subtracting, which means to take away. Then count how many are left.

GOAL 3

Cross out three of the animals in each box to subtract them. Then count the animals left in the box. **Remember**: Do not count the animals that have an X.

bear

How many bears are left?

rabbit

How many rabbits are left?

Read the poem below. Then write the word to finish the poem.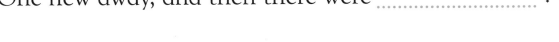

I saw four birds in a tree.
One flew away, and then there were 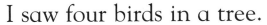 .

GOAL

Add together groups to make sets of ten.

Draw a line from the group in the first column to the group in the second column that makes a set of ten.

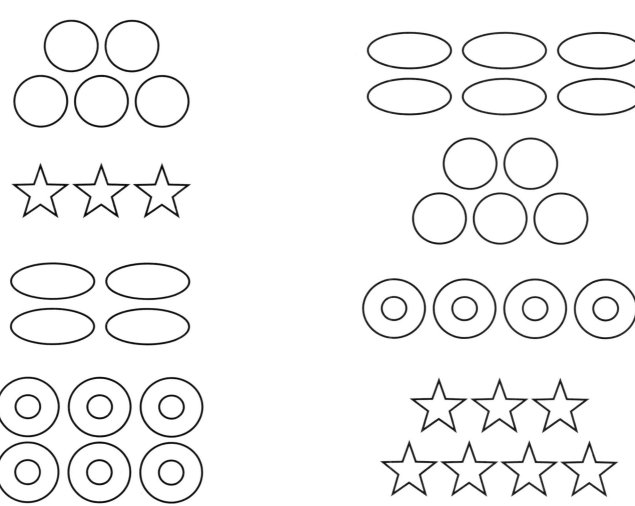

Circle a set of ten crayons below.

1234567891234567891

GOAL

Learn to sort items into groups that are the same.

Draw a line to match the number on each child's shirt to the numbers on the flags below.

Count all of the children on this page. How many are there?

GOAL

Learn to match sets and find pairs.

Look at these socks. Find and match the correct pairs.

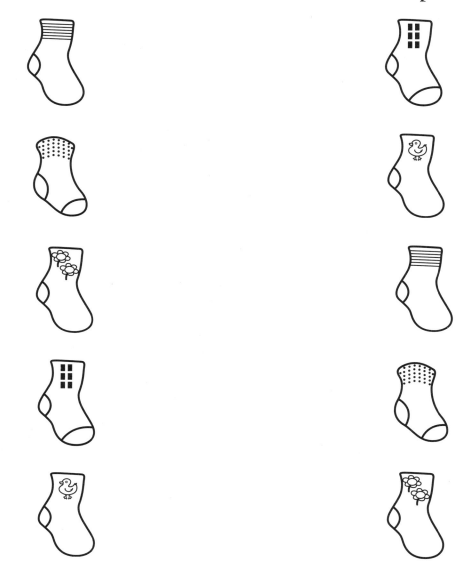

How many sets, or pairs, of socks are there above?
Circle the correct number.

5   6   8

Count to find the number of things in each set.

Count the farm animals in each box below. Then write the correct number of animals next to each box.

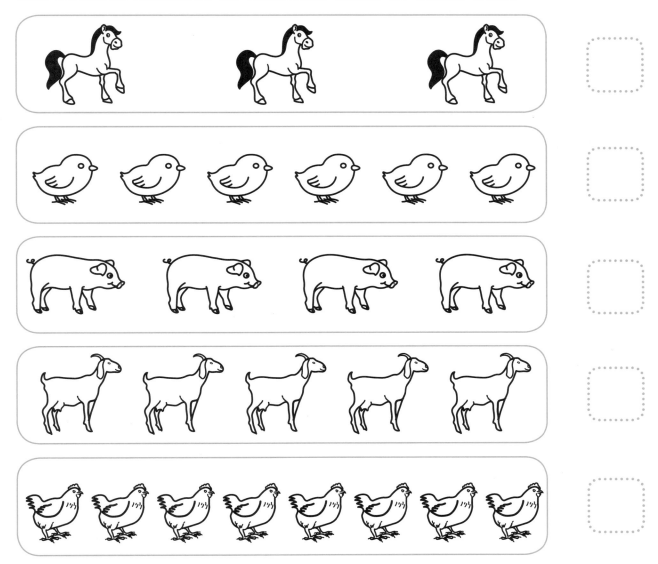

Count the chickens and the chicks. How many are there altogether? Circle the correct number.

7   14   16

GOAL

Compare the sizes of two objects to find the biggest.

Circle the biggest animal in each row below.

Draw a bigger turtle
in the box.

Learn to draw objects that are bigger or smaller.

Look at each picture, and follow the directions.

Draw a bigger sun.

Draw a bigger flower.

Draw a smaller star.

GOAL

Compare the lengths of two objects to find which is shorter and which is longer.

Look at each row carefully. Follow the directions.

Circle the longer snake.

Circle the shorter penguin.

Circle the horse with the shorter tail.

Circle the animal with the longer legs.

Circle the girl whose hair is longer.

Learn to draw objects that are longer or shorter.

Look at each picture. Follow the directions for each.

Longer

Draw a fish that is longer.

Shorter

Draw a bird with a shorter beak.

Look at the snake. How many dots long is this snake?
Count the dots, and circle the correct number.

● ● ● ● ● ● ● ● ● ● ● ● ● ● ● ● ● ● ● ●

12   18   20

GOAL

Compare the weights of objects to find the heaviest.

Which weighs more? Circle the heavier object in each box.

Meg's cat weighs 9 pounds.
Her dog weighs 15 pounds.
Which weighs more?

....

123456789123456789 12

Learn to draw things that are heavier or lighter.

Look at the mouse below. In the empty box, draw
an animal that is heavier than a mouse.

Look at the elephant below. In the empty box, draw
an animal that is lighter than an elephant.

Look at the three animals.
Circle the animal that
is the heaviest.

Learn position words, which tell us where an object is placed.

Look at the picture below. Circle the words to answer each question.

Where is the squirrel?	next to the tree	up in the tree
Where is the bird's nest?	below the tree branch	on the tree branch
Where are the children?	up in the tree	in front of the tree

Look at the insects below. Which one is in the middle? Circle the insect in the middle.

Review position words:

inside	outside	above
below	on	under

Look at the picture below. Circle the answer to each question.

Where is the cat?	inside the basket	outside the basket
Where is the dog?	above the table	below the table
Where is the bird?	inside the cage	outside the cage
Where is the cake?	under the table	on the table

GOAL

Learn to tell the time. A clock has two hands. The hour hand is short. The minute hand is long. The hour hand on this clock points to 3. The minute hand points to 12. That means the time is 3 o'clock.

3 o'clock

What time is shown on the clocks below?

☐ o'clock

☐ o'clock

☐ o'clock

☐ o'clock

Draw the hour hand on the clock to show 2 o'clock.

Remember: The hour hand is shorter than the minute hand.

1 2 3 4 5 6 7 8 9 1 2 3 4 5 6 7 8 9 1 2

Practice using clocks. When you write the word *o'clock*, that means the minute hand on the clock is pointing to 12. The hour hand points to the hour number.

Draw the hour hand on the clocks below to show the time that is under the clock.

Remember: The hour hand is shorter than the minute hand.

5 o'clock

2 o'clock

9 o'clock

6 o'clock

This clock is missing four numbers. Write the missing numbers in their correct places on the clock.

GOAL

Learn the concept of using money to buy items.

Draw a line from each toy to the dollars that match the price of the toy.

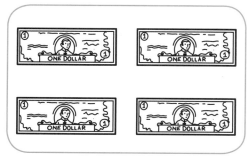

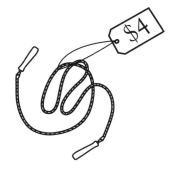

The price for a small jar of marbles is 3 dollars. The price for a large jar of marbles is 4 dollars. How many more dollars is the large jar?

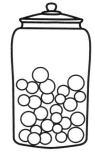

Count coins and bills to find the total amount of money.

Count the money in each pocket. Draw a line from each pocket to the correct amount written in the middle column.

10 cents

6 cents

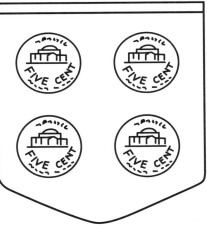

25 cents

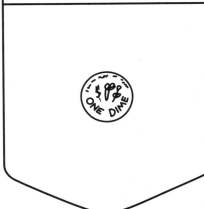

2 cents

1 dollar

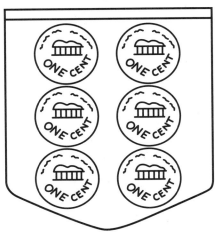

20 cents

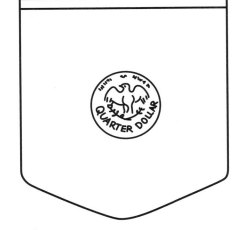

Certificate

Congratulations to

....

for successfully finishing this book.

K

Grade

GOOD JOB!

You're a star.

Date

....

Answer Section
with Parents' Notes

This book is intended to assist children studying math at the Kindergarten level. The math covered will be similar to what children are taught before and during Kindergarten programs.

Contents

By working through this book, your child will practice:
- reading, writing, counting, and adding to 20;
- finding more than, less than, and fewer than;
- recognizing differences and similarities;
- completing patterns and describing, comparing, and drawing shapes;
- measuring and comparing quantity, size, length, and width of objects;
- subtracting, or taking away one and more than one;
- sorting objects into sets, adding sets, and finding totals;
- using positional words, such as *top*, *bottom*, *above*, *below*, and others;
- drawing larger and heavier objects;
- telling and writing the time;
- recognizing money and counting coins.

How to Help Your Child

Your child's reading ability may not be up to the level of some of the more advanced math words, so be prepared to assist. Working with your child also has great benefits in helping you understand how he or she is thinking and reasoning, so that areas of difficulty for your child can be more easily determined.

Often, similar problems and concepts will be worded in different ways such as "count one more" and "which has more?" This is intentional and meant to make children aware that the same basic concepts can be expressed in different ways.

When appropriate, use props to help your child visualize solutions—for example, have a collection of coins to use for the money problems, or find examples of objects to measure around your house.

Build children's confidence with words of praise. If they are getting answers wrong, then encourage them to try again another time.

Good luck, and remember to have fun!

4

★ Count 1 to 5

Practice counting from 1 to 5.   1 2 3 4 5

How many stars are there in each row?
Circle the correct number.

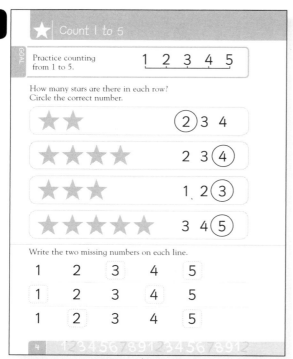

★ ★   (2) 3 4

★ ★ ★ ★   2 3 (4)

★ ★ ★   1 2 (3)

★ ★ ★ ★ ★   3 4 (5)

Write the two missing numbers on each line.

1	2	3	4	5
1	2	3	4	5
1	2	3	4	5

Let children count as they place a finger on each star. Then ask them to write the number under or on each star as they count, which will help reinforce their counting skills.

Count 6 to 10 ★

Practice counting from 6 to 10.   6 7 8 9 10

How many apples are there in each row?
Circle the correct number.

5 6 (7)

(6) 7 8

5 (8) 9

6 8 (10)

Circle any ten flowers below.   Answers may vary

Many children enjoy learning while touching or moving objects. Extend the activity on this page by providing cut-out paper apples that can be counted along with each row of apples on the page.

★ Count Up to 15

Practice counting from 10 to 15.   10 11 12 13 14 15

How many objects are there in each box?
Write the correct number.

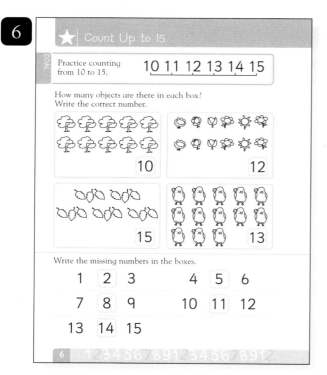

10   12

15   13

Write the missing numbers in the boxes.

1 2 3   4 5 6

7 8 9   10 11 12

13 14 15

To reinforce counting in groups, arrange twenty pennies into groups of two, four, six, and eight. Let children practice counting the pennies in each group, followed by adding up the numbers to find the total number of pennies.

Count Up to 20 ★

Practice counting up to 20.   15 16 17 18 19 20

Look at the twenty houses along the trail. Write the numbers that are missing in the circle next to each house.

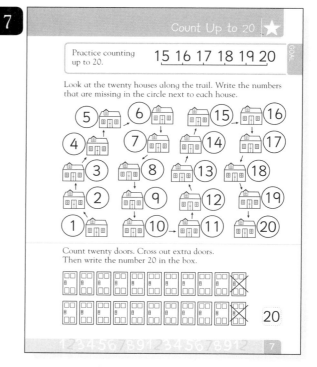

Count twenty doors. Cross out extra doors.
Then write the number 20 in the box.

20

Children will have fun following the trail as they count and write the missing numbers. Point to the numbers and explain that numbers increase by one on each step of the trail.

★ What Makes 10?

Add different numbers from 1 to 9 to make 10.

Count each group of toys. Write the correct number of toys in the box.

10

10

10

10

Copy the pattern of dots on the other side of the domino.

Now count all the dots on the domino, and write the correct number.

10

Encourage children to look for patterns to help them determine quantities and gain confidence in their math skills. For example, three and three should become instantly recognizable as six. Let them move objects to match the patterns on the page.

9

Practice Making 10 ★

Review how to make 10.

Write the numbers from 1 to 10 in the circles next to each car on the path below.

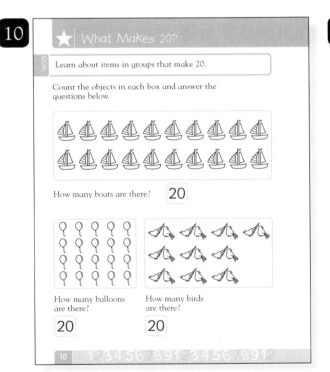

Learning what makes ten is key to understanding our number system. Try the following exercise: Cut out ten circles. Label each circle with a number and a corresponding series of dots. Have children practice selecting groups of circles that make ten.

10

★ What Makes 20?

Learn about items in groups that make 20.

Count the objects in each box and answer the questions below.

How many boats are there? 20

How many balloons are there? 20

How many birds are there? 20

Draw a row of twenty squares. Number each square from 1 to 20, and let children see and count the numbers. Then cut out twenty cardboard circles, and let children arrange them in groups to see how many ways they can make twenty—four groups of five, a group of four and two groups of eight, and so on.

Practice Making 20 ★

Review ways to make 20, such as 10 + 10.

Solve these equations.

6 + 14 = 20   9 + 11 = 20   8 + 12 = 20

5 + 15 = 20   3 + 17 = 20   16 + 4 = 20

13 + 7 = 20   18 + 2 = 20   19 + 1 = 20

Circle the equation that adds up to 20.

12 + 4 + 6   (5 + 5 + 10)   4 + 4 + 9

Follow the path to the castle and write the missing numbers on each stone.

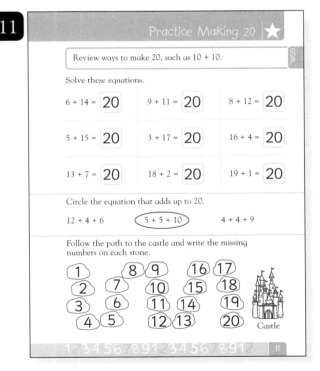

Have fun playing a game: Create a set of twenty cards, and number them 1 through 20. Create another set of twenty cards, but this time use star stickers to represent the numbers. Let children match each number card with its corresponding star-sticker card.

★ Recognize Shapes

GOAL Learn that objects have shapes, and shapes have names.

Look at the objects. Circle the correct shape of the object in each row.

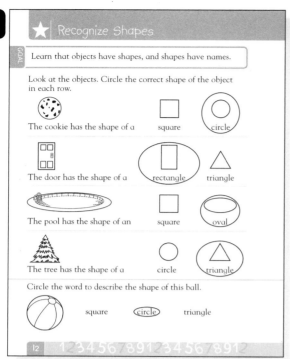

The cookie has the shape of a   square   circle

The door has the shape of a   rectangle   triangle

The pool has the shape of an   square   oval

The tree has the shape of a   circle   triangle

Circle the word to describe the shape of this ball.

square   circle   triangle

Help children identify shapes. After reading a picture book, review the pages and point out circles, squares, and triangles in the illustrations. Take turns as you look at each page to see how many shapes you can find in each scene.

13

Different Shapes ★

GOAL Learn to identify different shapes.

Look at the shapes in each row. Circle the shape that is different.

Draw five triangles below. Then draw a silly face on each one.

Answers may vary

Reinforce problem-solving skills in creative ways. After baking a pan of brownies, let children help decide how you will cut them up. Let your child estimate how many servings of brownies you can cut.

14

★ Describe Shapes

GOAL Describe shapes by the number of sides and corners.

Circle the word that correctly completes each sentence.

A square has four corners and _____ sides.   three   four

A circle is _____ .   round   straight

A rectangle has four corners and is _____ .   round   long

A triangle has three corners and _____ sides.   two   three

Circle the triangle that is larger than the others.

Make a simple jigsaw puzzle to reinforce shapes: Cut up the front of an old cereal box or an old greeting card into circles, squares, triangles, and rectangles. Engage children in describing the shapes as they work to put the puzzle together.

Compare Shapes ★

GOAL Shapes can vary in size. Learn to find the shapes that are larger.

Look at the shapes in each box. Color in the largest shape.

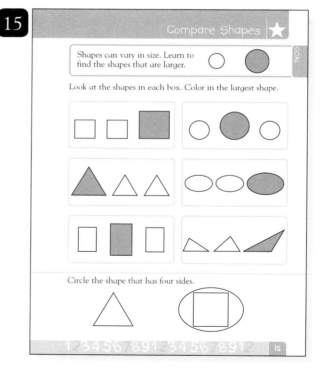

Circle the shape that has four sides.

Cut scrap paper into a variety of shapes and sizes. Guide children in sorting the paper first by shapes, and then into size order. You can provide plastic containers for easy sorting.

★ Create Shapes

GOAL Learn to draw shapes.

Look at each shape and make it into an object.

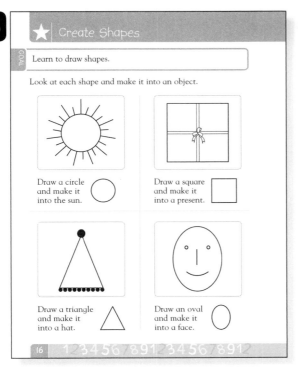

Draw a circle and make it into the sun. ◯

Draw a square and make it into a present. ▢

Draw a triangle and make it into a hat. △

Draw an oval and make it into a face. ◯

Encourage shape skills and tactile learning with colorful clay: Provide children with four lumps of colored clay. Ask them to form a circle, a square, a triangle, and an oval using the clay.

17

More Shapes ★

GOAL Practice finding and counting shapes.

Color the circles red. ◯ Color the rectangles yellow. ▭
Color the squares blue. ▢ Color the triangles green. △

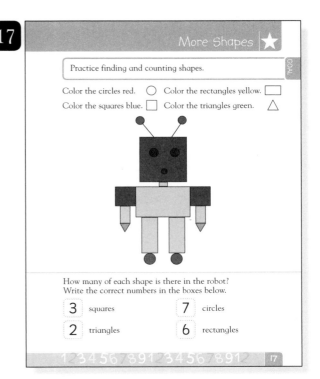

How many of each shape is there in the robot? Write the correct numbers in the boxes below.

3 squares   **7** circles

2 triangles   **6** rectangles

Guide children in using the key. Color each shape in the key to illustrate how they should color the shapes on the robot. Review as they begin to color to check their understanding.

18

★ Shape Patterns

GOAL Learn to draw shapes and continue patterns. Patterns are repeated sets of objects.

Draw the shape to continue the pattern in each row.

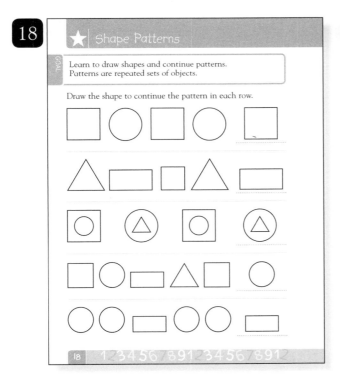

To extend their knowledge of shapes, ask children to draw a picture of their room, a toy, or the playground. Encourage them to use shapes in their drawing. Review their drawings, and ask them to point to and name the shapes.

19

More Patterns ★

GOAL Practice continuing patterns.

Look at the cupcakes below. In each row, follow the pattern and decorate the tops of the undecorated cupcakes with the correct design.

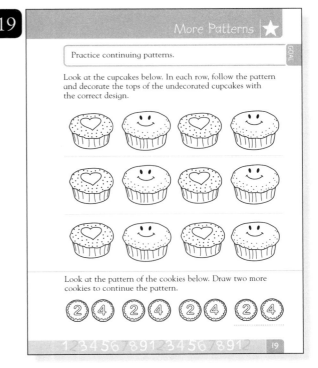

Look at the pattern of the cookies below. Draw two more cookies to continue the pattern.

Have fun and reinforce math skills by using stickers. Start a simple pattern and let them continue it. Then have them create a pattern of either the shapes or colors of the stickers.

★ The Same

Learn to identify objects that are the same.

Look at each row of animals. Circle the two animals that are the same.

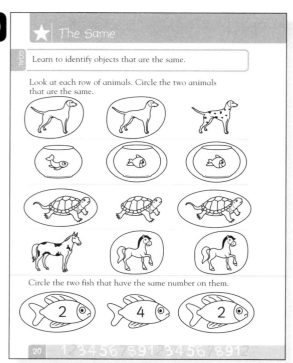

Circle the two fish that have the same number on them.

Reinforce accuracy of numbers. Write the numbers from 1 to 20 on scraps of paper. Include four numbers that are written incorrectly, backward, or missing a part. Ask children to find the numbers that are not correct.

Which Has the Same? ★

Learn to compare characteristics, such as numbers and letters.

Put the balls into the correct boxes: Draw a line from each ball with a number on it to the number box. Draw a line from each ball with a letter on it to the letter box.

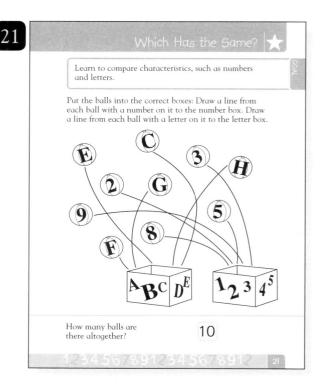

How many balls are there altogether?   10

Many children need help determining the difference between letters and numbers, and the difference between numbers and letters that look similar—6 and 9, 1 and 7, E and F, and so on. The activity on this page will reinforce those skills.

★ Not the Same

Learn to find things that are not the same, or different.

Circle the leaf in each row that is different.

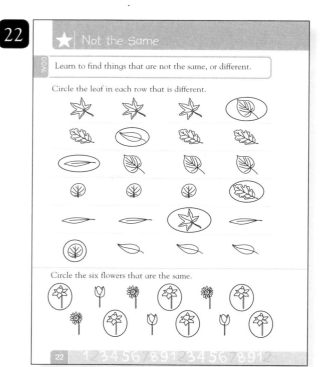

Circle the six flowers that are the same.

Let children help with gardening or caring for houseplants. Reinforce classifying flowers and leaves that are the same and different. This helps build observation skills, which are important in learning math.

Which is Different? ★

Learn to identify (spot) which is different.

Circle the animal in each row that is different.

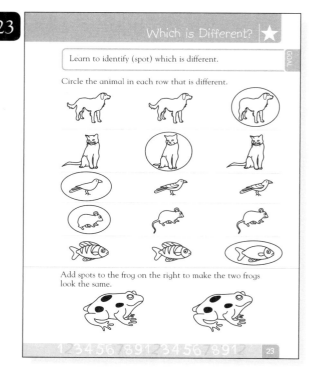

Add spots to the frog on the right to make the two frogs look the same.

Read an illustrated book about animals with your child. Ask questions like, "What is different about those fish?" and "What is the same about these bears?" Describing what is different and what is the same helps children learn to compare things.

★ Which Has More?

Count the objects to find out which set has more.

Write the letter **M** on the line under the box that has more objects.

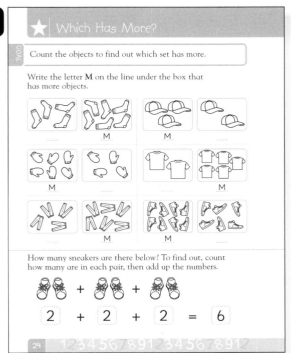

How many sneakers are there below? To find out, count how many are in each pair, then add up the numbers.

2 + 2 + 2 = 6

Encourage children to identify quantity by looking at objects without counting them. This introduces the skill of estimating. Display two jars of coins, one nearly full and one half full, and ask: "Which jar has more coins?"

Add One More ★

Learn to add one more.

Add one more to each group in the boxes. Then count the total items in the group and write the correct number.

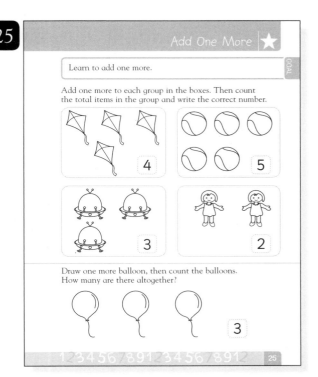

Draw one more balloon, then count the balloons. How many are there altogether?

3

Tell a simple story and draw simple pictures to reinforce adding. Here is an example: "Amy had two cookies. Adam gave her one more. How many cookies does Amy have now?"

★ Add More

Draw more shapes to add to the group. The + sign means to add. ○ + ○○ = 3

Draw two more of the same shape in each box. Then add all the shapes and write the correct number.

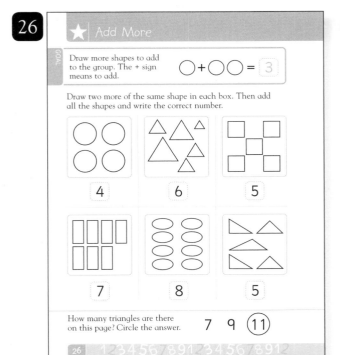

How many triangles are there on this page? Circle the answer. 7 9 ⑪

Use the activities on this page to reinforce adding skills. Introduce the addition sign (+) by using it when helping children to write out the addition problems involved in adding more shapes to each box.

How Many in Total? ★

Find the total, which is the answer you get when you add things together. ☁ + ☁☁ = 6

Draw a + sign between the boxes in each row. Then count all the items in both of the boxes and write the total number.

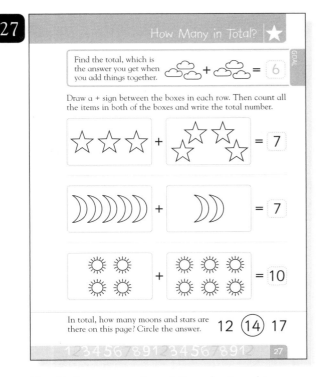

= 7

= 7

= 10

In total, how many moons and stars are there on this page? Circle the answer. 12 ⑭ 17

Combining sets can be reinforced using objects such as plastic toys or buttons. Arrange objects in small groups according to shape or color. Let children sort groups and gain an understanding of sorting and sets.

★ Which Has Fewer?

Find the group that has fewer objects.

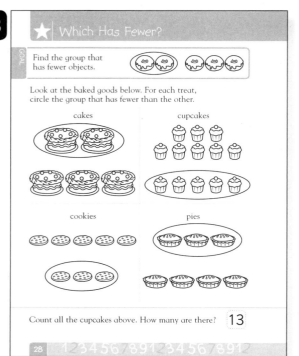

Look at the baked goods below. For each treat, circle the group that has fewer than the other.

cakes

cupcakes

cookies

pies

Count all the cupcakes above. How many are there? **13**

Guide children in looking for the group with fewer items. Model how to count the cakes in each group. Ask: "Which group has fewer cakes? Which group has more?"

Take Away One ★

Take away one object so that a group has one fewer. 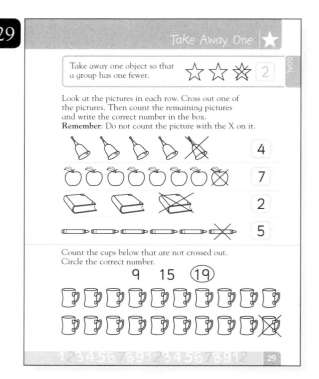 **2**

Look at the pictures in each row. Cross out one of the pictures. Then count the remaining pictures and write the correct number in the box.
Remember: Do not count the picture with the X on it.

4

7

2

5

Count the cups below that are not crossed out. Circle the correct number.

9   15   (19)

Introduce the concept of taking away, or subtracting, with a simple story. For example, "Tim had three toy cars. Tony took one car. How many cars did Tim have left?" Use toy cars to model the story.

★ Take Away More

Cross out to show taking away more than one. Count to find how many are left. 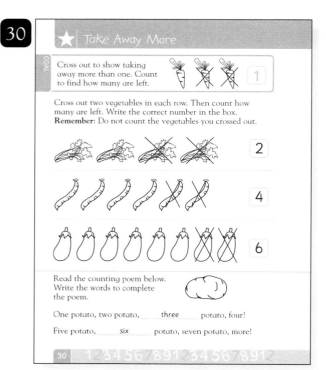 **1**

Cross out two vegetables in each row. Then count how many are left. Write the correct number in the box.
Remember: Do not count the vegetables you crossed out.

2

4

6

Read the counting poem below. Write the words to complete the poem.

One potato, two potato, ___three___ potato, four!

Five potato, ___six___ potato, seven potato, more!

Children may need hands-on objects to be able to comprehend taking objects away and counting what's left. Use toys or plastic blocks to act out the activities on the page and to be sure children understand the basic idea of subtraction.

Subtract ★

Practice subtracting, which means to take away. Then count how many are left. 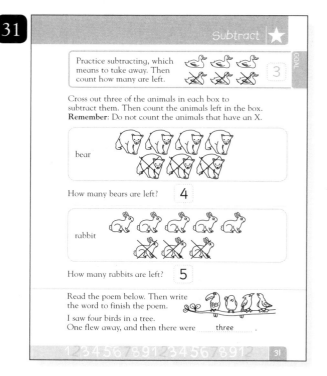 **3**

Cross out three of the animals in each box to subtract them. Then count the animals left in the box.
Remember: Do not count the animals that have an X.

bear

How many bears are left? **4**

rabbit

How many rabbits are left? **5**

Read the poem below. Then write the word to finish the poem.
I saw four birds in a tree.
One flew away, and then there were ___three___ .

Point to the sample problem to make sure children know what to do. Let them count the animals that remain after making an X on three animals. Then ask: "How many animals will be left if you take away three?"

★ Sorting Objects into Sets

GOAL: Add together groups to make sets of ten.

Draw a line from the group in the first column to the group in the second column that makes a set of ten.

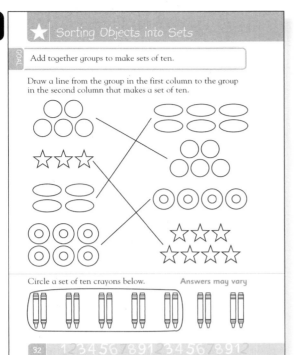

Circle a set of ten crayons below.　　Answers may vary

Reinforce counting, sets, and shapes. Cut cardboard into shapes, making sets of ten of each shape. Place them in a container. Engage children in taking them out of the container one at a time and sorting them by shape. Add a challenge by asking them to create special sets, sets of five or two.

Which Group? ★

GOAL: Learn to sort items into groups that are the same.

Draw a line to match the number on each child's shirt to the numbers on the flags below.

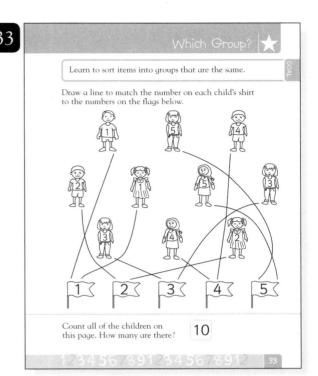

Count all of the children on this page. How many are there? **10**

To extend the activity on the page, make a box under each flag. Together, count the children matched to each flag and write the correct number in each box.

★ How Many Sets?

GOAL: Learn to match sets and find pairs.

Look at these socks. Find and match the correct pairs.

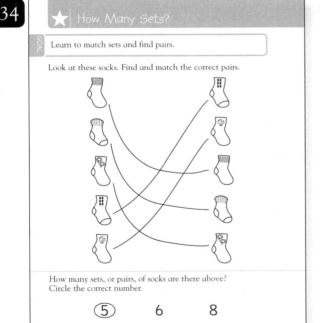

How many sets, or pairs, of socks are there above? Circle the correct number.

⑤　　6　　8

Identifying sets helps children use the observation skills they also need in reading, science, and other areas of the curriculum. Finding and matching sets also helps children begin to develop problem-solving skills.

Counting Sets ★

GOAL: Count to find the number of things in each set.

Count the farm animals in each box below. Then write the correct number of animals next to each box.

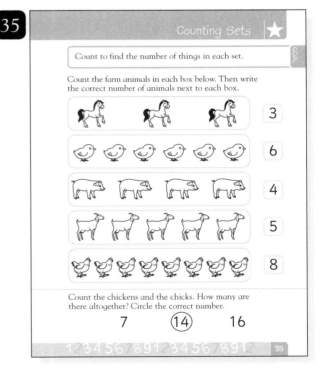

3

6

4

5

8

Count the chickens and the chicks. How many are there altogether? Circle the correct number.

7　　⑭　　16

Once children understand counting, challenge them by asking questions that require them to add two groups of objects. Use the activity on this page for prompts. Ask: "How many pigs and goats are there in all?"; "How many chicks and horses are there altogether?"

★ Compare Size

Compare the sizes of two objects to find the biggest.

Circle the biggest animal in each row below.

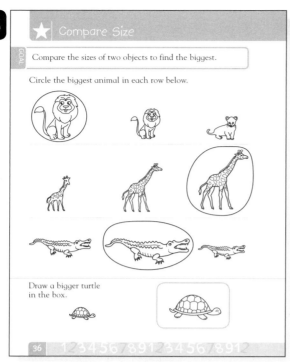

Draw a bigger turtle in the box.

Reinforce size and comparison by using pictures and key vocabulary words. Ask children questions to compare size: "Which animal in this row is the smallest?"; "Which animal in this row is bigger than the smallest one, and smaller than the biggest one?"

Draw Bigger or Smaller ★

Learn to draw objects that are bigger or smaller.

Look at each picture, and follow the directions.

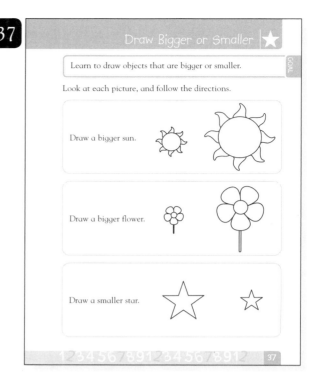

Draw a bigger sun.

Draw a bigger flower.

Draw a smaller star.

Encourage children to draw to help them learn to compare sizes. This requires little direction and lets children experiment as they develop independence in solving problems. They will also learn to use words related to size and shape.

★ Compare Length

Compare the lengths of two objects to find which is shorter and which is longer.

Look at each row carefully. Follow the directions.

Circle the longer snake.

Circle the shorter penguin.

Circle the horse with the shorter tail.

Circle the animal with the longer legs.

Circle the girl whose hair is longer.

Ask questions about length while children are working with blocks or modeling clay. Make rows of blocks or roll out pieces of clay to different lengths. Ask: "Which is the longest?"; "Which is the shortest?"

Draw Longer or Shorter ★

Learn to draw objects that are longer or shorter.

Look at each picture. Follow the directions for each.

Longer

Draw a fish that is longer.   Answers may vary

Shorter

Draw a bird with a shorter beak.   Answers may vary

Look at the snake. How many dots long is this snake? Count the dots, and circle the correct number.

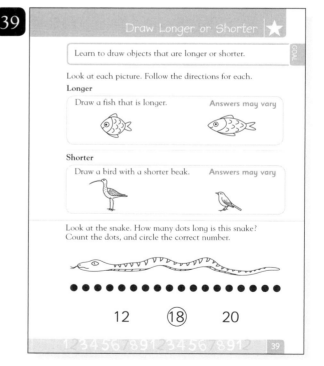

12   (18)   20

Show children how to estimate length. Display pieces of colorful yarn or strips of paper. Ask children to place them in order of length from the shortest to the longest.

★ Compare Weight

Compare the weights of objects to find the heaviest.

Which weighs more? Circle the heavier object in each box.

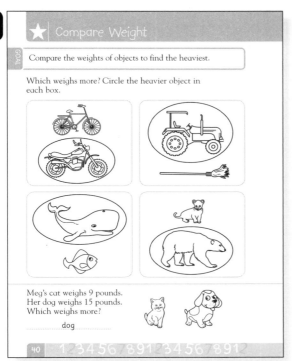

Meg's cat weighs 9 pounds.
Her dog weighs 15 pounds.
Which weighs more?

.... dog

Discuss with children different tools used to weigh things, such as the bathroom scale, the kitchen scale, and the scale at the supermarket. Let children use a small kitchen scale to weigh toys, dolls, or amounts of food.

Draw Heavier or Lighter ★

Learn to draw things that are heavier or lighter.

Look at the mouse below. In the empty box, draw an animal that is heavier than a mouse.

Look at the elephant below. In the empty box, draw an animal that is lighter than an elephant.

Answers may vary

Answers may vary

Look at the three animals. Circle the animal that is the heaviest.

Most children have prior knowledge about animals; though they may never have seen certain real animals, they have acquired knowledge from seeing animals in books and other places. Ask questions like, "How do you know that a horse is heavier than a chick?"

★ Position

Learn position words, which tell us where an object is placed.

Look at the picture below. Circle the words to answer each question.

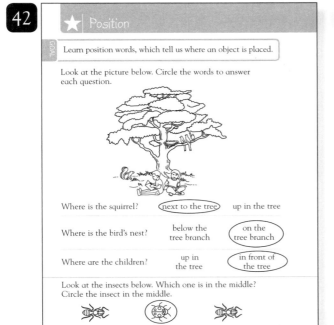

Where is the squirrel?   (next to the tree)   up in the tree

Where is the bird's nest?   below the tree branch   (on the tree branch)

Where are the children?   up in the tree   (in front of the tree)

Look at the insects below. Which one is in the middle? Circle the insect in the middle.

Children may need help reading the questions and answers on this page. Read them aloud if necessary. Then solicit responses. It may be helpful to ask children to point to the picture and then respond with the correct position words.

More Positions ★

Review position words:

inside   outside   above
     below   on   under

Look at the picture below. Circle the answer to each question.

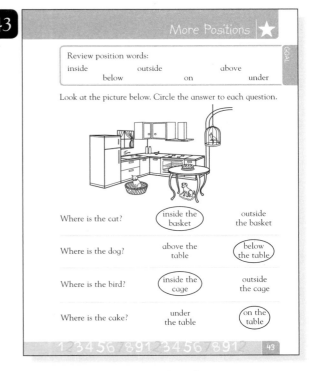

Where is the cat?   (inside the basket)   outside the basket

Where is the dog?   above the table   (below the table)

Where is the bird?   (inside the cage)   outside the cage

Where is the cake?   under the table   (on the table)

See if children can respond to the questions without reading the possible answers. Ask questions to encourage children to use the position words, and point to the correct answer, reading it aloud. This will help them make connections between pictures and words.

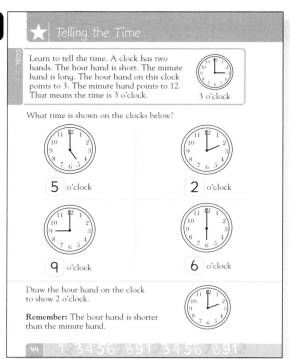

★ Telling the Time

GOAL Learn to tell the time. A clock has two hands. The hour hand is short. The minute hand is long. The hour hand on this clock points to 3. The minute hand points to 12. That means the time is 3 o'clock.

3 o'clock

What time is shown on the clocks below?

5 o'clock

2 o'clock

9 o'clock

6 o'clock

Draw the hour hand on the clock to show 2 o'clock.

Remember: The hour hand is shorter than the minute hand.

Incorporate time into daily conversations with children. Point to a clock, and say, "We have to get up at 7 o'clock tomorrow morning." Then ask, "Where will the hour hand be pointing at 7 o'clock?"

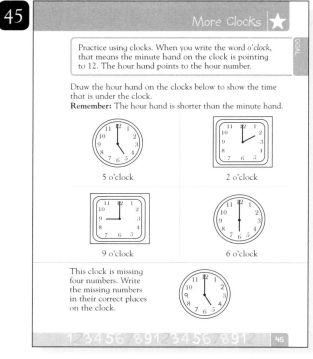

More Clocks ★

GOAL Practice using clocks. When you write the word *o'clock*, that means the minute hand on the clock is pointing to 12. The hour hand points to the hour number.

Draw the hour hand on the clocks below to show the time that is under the clock.
Remember: The hour hand is shorter than the minute hand.

5 o'clock

2 o'clock

9 o'clock

6 o'clock

This clock is missing four numbers. Write the missing numbers in their correct places on the clock.

Tell children that the analog clocks shown on this page, with hands that point to the time, are only one kind of clock. Explain that there are also digital clocks that are used on computers, cell phones, and alarm clocks. Digital clocks have no hands; they display numbers to tell you the time in hours and minutes.

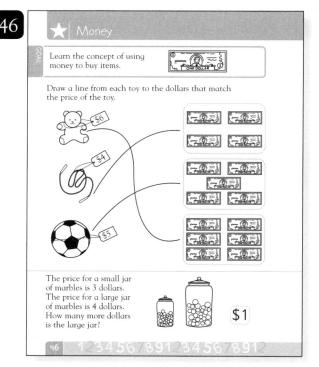

★ Money

GOAL Learn the concept of using money to buy items.

ONE DOLLAR

Draw a line from each toy to the dollars that match the price of the toy.

$6

$4

$5

The price for a small jar of marbles is 3 dollars. The price for a large jar of marbles is 4 dollars. How many more dollars is the large jar?

$1

As children match written dollar amounts with the quantity of dollars shown in the right-hand column, they will become familiar with counting and recognizing amounts of money. Let children act out buying toys with fake paper dollars you create together, or fake paper dollars from a board game.

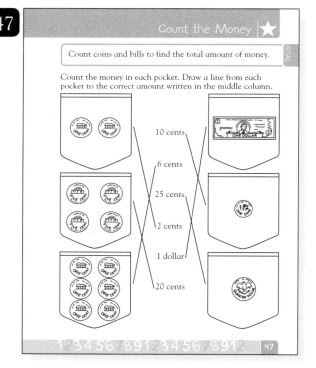

Count the Money ★

GOAL Count coins and bills to find the total amount of money.

Count the money in each pocket. Draw a line from each pocket to the correct amount written in the middle column.

10 cents

6 cents

25 cents

2 cents

1 dollar

20 cents

This activity will help reinforce children's ability to count money and recognize the value of both paper money and coins. Having coins and paper money on hand may be helpful. Let children count real coins to match the quantities listed on the page.